Walter Crane, Edmund Evans

The baby's bouquet:

A fresh bunch of old rhymes & tunes

Walter Crane, Edmund Evans

The baby's bouquet:
A fresh bunch of old rhymes & tunes

ISBN/EAN: 9783744637855

Printed in Europe, USA, Canada, Australia, Japan

Cover: Foto ©Thomas Meinert / pixelio.de

More available books at **www.hansebooks.com**

THE BABY'S BOUQUET

A FRESH BUNCH OF OLD RHYMES & TUNES

A COMPANION TO THE BABY'S OPERA

THE TUNES COLLECTED & ARRANGED BY L.C.

ENGRAVED & WALTER CRANE DECORATED BY

CUT & PRINTED BY EDMUND IN COLOURS EVANS

LONDON & NEW YORK
GEORGE ROUTLEDGE
AND SONS

THE BABY'S BOUQUET

To

THE FRIENDS OF BABIES,

AND OF "BABY'S OPERA",

IN ENGLAND, AMERICA, & ELSEWHERE.

CONTENTS

POLLY PUT·THE KETTLE ON

Pol-ly, put the ket-tle on, Pol-ly, put the ket-tle on, Pol-ly, put the

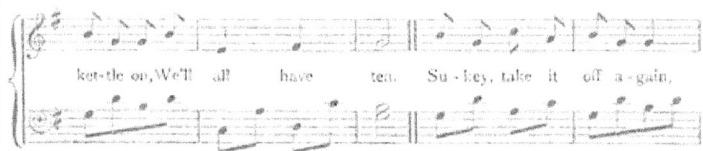

ket-tle on, We'll all have tea. Su-key, take it off a-gain,

Su-key, take it off a-gain, Su-key, take it off again, They've all gone a-way.

HOT CROSS BUONS

Hot Cross Buns! Hot Cross Buns! One a penny, two a penny, Hot Cross Buns!

If you have no daugh-ters, If you have no daugh-ters, If you have no

daugh-ters, Pray give them to your sons; But if you have none of

these lit-tle elves, Then you must eat them all your-selves.

THE · LITTLE · WOMAN

There was a lit-tle woman, as I've heard say, Fol, lol, did-dle, did-dle dol ;

She went to mar-ket, her eggs for to sell, Fol, lol, did-dle, did-dle dol.

She went to market all on a market day, And she fell a-sleep up-on the king's highway ;

'AND·THE·PEDLAR'

Fol de rol de lol lol, lol lol lol, Fol, lol, did-dle, did-dle dol.

2 And there came a pedlar whose name was Stout,
   Fol, lol, &c.,
He cut her petticoats all round about,
   Fol, lol, &c.,
He cut her petticoats up to her knees,
Which made the little woman to shiver and freeze.
   Fol de rol, &c.,

3 When the little woman began to awake,
   Fol, lol, &c.,
She began to shiver, and she began to shake,
   Fol, lol, &c.,
She began to shake, and she began to cry,
Lawk-a-mercy on me! this is none of I,
   Fol de rol, &c.,

4 If it be I, as I suppose it be,
   Fol lol, &c.,
I've a little dog at home, and he knows me;
   Fol, lol, &c.,
If it be I, he will wag his little tail,
If it be not I, he will bark and rail,
   Fol de rol, &c.,

5 And when the little woman went home in the dark,
   Fol, lol, &c.,
Her little dog he did begin to bark,
   Fol, lol, &c.,
He began to bark, and she began to cry,
Lawk-a-mercy on me! this is none of I,
   Fol de rol, &c.,

✠ THE ✠ LITTLE ✠ DISASTER ✠

Once there lived a lit-tle man, Where a lit-tle ri-ver ran, And he
had a lit-tle farm and lit-tle dai-ry O! And he had a lit-tle plough, And a
lit-tle dap-pled cow, Which he of-ten called his pret-ty lit-tle Fai-ry O!

2 And his dog he called Fidelle,
  For he loved his master well;
And he had a little pony for his pleasure O!
  In a sty not very big
  He'd a frisky little pig,
Which he often called his little piggy treasure O!

3 Once his little maiden, Ann,
  With her pretty little can,
Went a-milking when the morning sun was beam-
      ing O!
  When she fell, I don't know how,
  But she stumbled o'er the plough,
And the cow was quite astonished at her scream-
      ing O!

4 Little maid cried out in vain,
  While the milk ran o'er the plain,
Little pig ran grunting after it so guily O!
  While the little dog behind,
  For a share was much inclined,
So he pulled back squeaking piggy by the tail O!

5 Such a clatter now began
  As alarmed the little man,
Who came capering from out his little stable O!
  Pony trod on doggy's toes,
  Doggy snapped at piggy's nose,
Piggy made as great a noise as he was able O!

6 Then to make the story short,
  Little pony with a snort
Lifted up his little heels so very clever O!
  And the man he tumbled down,
  And he neatly cracked his crown,
And this only made the matter worse than ever O!

THE OLD WOMAN OF NORWICH

There was an old wo-man and what do you think? She
lived up-on nothing but vic-tuals and drink; Vic-tuals and drink were the
chief of her diet, Yet this pla-guey old wo-man could ne-ver be quiet.

THE OLD WOMAN TOSSED UP IN A BLANKET

There was an old woman tossed up in a blanket, Seventeen times as high as the moon; Where she was going I could not but ask it, For in her hand she carried a broom. "Old woman, old woman, old woman," quoth I; "O whither, O whither, O whither so high?" "To sweep the cobwebs from the sky, And I'll be with you by-and-by!"

BUY A BROOM

From Deutsch-land I come with my light wares all la-den, To

dear.... hap-py Eng-land in summer's gay bloom; Then lis-ten, fair

la-dy, and young pret-ty mädchen, Come buy of the wan-der-ing

Baier-in a broom; A large one for the la-dy, and a small one for the

ba-by, Come buy ye, pret-ty la-dy, come buy ye a broom.

HAUSEGEFINDE

Wi - de - wi - de - wen - ne heisst mei - ne Putt - hen - ne,

Kann-nicht-ruhn heisst mein Huhn, Wa - del-schwanz heisst mei - ne Gans;

Wi - de - wi - de - wen - ne heisst mei - ne Putt - hen - ne.

2 Widewidewenne heisst meine Putt-henne,
Entequent heisst meine Ent,
Snunnelmatz heisst meine Katz;
Widewidewenne heisst meine Putt-henne.

3 Widewidewenne heisst meine Putt-henne,
Schwartz und weiss heisst meine Geis,
Schmärtopflein heisst mein Schwein,
Widewidewenne heisst meine Putt-henne.

4 Widewidewenne heisst meine Putt-henne,
Ehrenwerth heisst mein Pferd,
Gute-Muh heisst meine Kuh;
Widewidewenne heisst meine Putt-henne.

5 Widewidewenne heisst meine Putt-henne,
Wettermann heisst mein Hahn,
Kunterbunt heisst mein Hund;
Widewidewenne heisst meine Putt-henne.

6 Widewidewenne heisst meine Putt-henne,
Gack-heraus heisst mein Haus,

Schlupf-heraus heisst mein Maus;
Widewidewenne heisst meine Putt-henne.

7 Widewidewenne heisst meine Putt-henne,
Wohlgethan heisst mein Mann,
Sausewind heisst mein Kind,
Widewidewenne heisst meine Putt-henne.

Gesprochen:
Nun kennt ihr mich mit Mann und Kind,
Und meinem ganzen Hausgesind.

SCHLAF, KINDLEIN, SCHLAF.

Schlaf, Kind-lein, schlaf, Draus-sen steht ein schaf, Stösst sich ein-em Stein-e-lein, That ihm weh das Bein-e-lein, Schlaf, Kindlein, schlaf. Schlaf, Kindlein, schlaf.

LITTLE·MAN·&·MAID

There was a lit-tle man And he woo'd a lit-tle maid, And he said, "Lit-tle maid, will you wed, wed, wed? I have lit-tle more to say Than 'will you, yea or nay?' For least said is soon-est men - ded - ded - ded - ded."

2 The little maid replied,
(Some say a little sighed,)
" But what shall we have to eat, eat, eat?
" Will the love that you're rich in
" Make a fire in the kitchen?
" Or the little god of love turn the spit, spit, spit?"

THE JOLLY TESTER

O dear Six-pence, i've got Six-pence, I love Six-pence as

I love my life; I'll spend a pen-ny on't, and

I'll lend an-o-ther on't, And I'll car-ry four-pence home to my wife.

2 O dear Four-pence, I've got Four-pence,
I love Four-pence as I love my life;
I'll spend a penny on't, and I'll lend an-
other on't,
And I'll carry two-pence home to my wife.

3 O dear Two-pence, I've got Two-pence,
I love Two-pence as I love my life;
I'll spend a penny on't, and I'll lend a penny
on't,
And I'll carry nothing home to my wife.

4 O dear nothing, I've got nothing,
What will nothing buy for my wife?
I have nothing, I spend nothing,
I love nothing better than my wife

24

LUCY · LOCKET

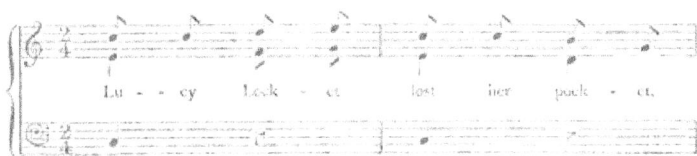

Lu - cy Lock - et lost her pock - et,

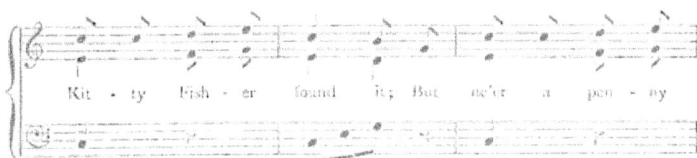

Kit - ty Fish - er found it; But ne'er a pen - ny

was there in't, Ex - cept the bind - ing round it.

If all the world were pa - per, And
all the sea were ink,...... And all the trees were
bread and cheese, What should we do for drink?

2 If all the world were sand—O!
Oh, then what should we lack—O!
If, as they say, there were no clay,
How should we take tobacco?

3 If all our vessels ran—a,
If none but had a crack,
If Spanish apes ate all the grapes,
How should we do for sack?

A ship, a ship a-sail - ing, A-sail - ing on the sea,.... And

it was deep-ly la - den With pret-ty things for me;.....

There were rai - sins in the ca - bin, And al-monds in the hold; The

sails were made of sa - tin, And the mast it was of gold.

2 The four-and-twenty sailors
That stood between the decks,
Were four-and-twenty white mice
With rings about their necks.

The captain was a duck, a duck,
With a jacket on his back,
And when this fairy ship set sail,
The captain he said " Quack!"

THE·LiTTLE·CoCK·SPARRoW

A lit-tle cock-sparrow sat on a high tree, A lit-tle cock-sparrow sat on a high tree, A lit-tle cock-spar-row sat on a high tree, And he chirrupped, he chirrupped so mer-ri-ly. He chirrupped, he chirrupped, he chirrupped, he chirrupped, He chirrupped, he chirrupped, he chirrupped, A lit-tle cock-sparrow sat on a high tree, And he chirrupped, he chirrupped so mer-ri-ly.

2 A naughty little boy with a bow and arrow,
Determined to shoot this little cock-sparrow;

3 For this little cock-sparrow would make a nice stew,
And his giblets would make a nice little pie too.

4 "Oh, no," says cock-sparrow, "I won't make a stew,"
And he fluttered his wings, and away he flew.

THE CARRION CROW

A car-rion crow sat on an oak, Der-ry, der-ry, der-ry,

dec - co; A car-rion crow sat on an oak, Watching a tai-lor

shaping his cloak. Heigh-ho! the car-rion crow, Der-ry, der-ry, der-ry, dec - co,

2 " O wife, bring me my old bent bow,"
 Derry, derry, derry, decco:
" O wife, bring me my old bent bow.
" That I may shoot yon carrion crow,"
 Heigh-ho! the carrion crow,
 Derry, derry, derry, decco.

3 The tailor shot, and he missed his mark,
 Derry, derry, derry, decco:
The tailor shot, and he missed his mark,
And shot his old sow right through the heart
 Heigh-ho! the carrion crow,
 Derry, derry, derry, decco.

" O wife, bring brandy in a spoon,
 Derry, derry, derry, decco:
" O wife, bring brandy in a spoon,
" For our old sow is in a swoon,"
 Heigh-ho! the carrion crow,
 Derry, derry, derry, decco.

THE SCARECROW

O all you lit-tle black-ey tops, Pray don't you eat my

fa-ther's crops, While I lie down to take a nap. Shu-

-a.............. O!...... Shu-a.............. O!......

2 If father he perchance should come,
With his cocked hat and his long gun,
Then you must fly and I must run.
Shua O! Shua O!

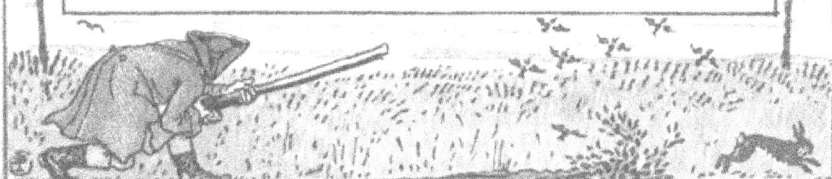

x
31

THE
NORTH & WIND
& THE ROBIN

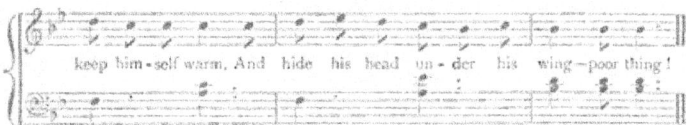

The north wind doth blow And we shall have snow, And
what will poor Rob-in do then—poor thing? He'll sit in a barn To
keep him-self warm, And hide his head un-der his wing—poor thing!

A, B, C, die Kat-ze lief in Schnee, Und

wie sie wie-der 'raus kam, Da hatt' sie weis-se Stief-lein an: O

je - mi-ne, O je - mi-ne, O je - mi-ne, O je!

2 A, B, C, die Katze lief zur Höh,'
Sie lecket ihr kalt Pfötchen rein
Und putzt sich auch das Stiefelein
Und ging nicht mehr in Schnee.

ET·MOI·DE· M'EN·COURIR

En pass-sant dans un p'tit bois, Où le cou-cou chan-tait, Où le cou-

cou, chan-tait; Dans son jo - li chant il di - sait Cou-cou, cou - cou, cou-cou, cou-

cou, Et moi qui croy-ais qu'il di - sait; Cass' lui le cou, cass' lui le

cou! Et moi de m'en cour', cour', cour'. Et moi de m'en cou - rir!

2 En passant auprès d'un étang
  Où les canards chantaient,
  Où les canards chantaient
  Dans leur joli chant ils disaient :
  " Cancan, cancan, cancan, cancan "
  Et moi qui croyais qu'ils disaient,
  " Jett' le dedans, jett' le dedans."
  Et moi de m'en cour', cour', cour'.
    Et moi de m'en courir !

3 En passant devant une maison,
  Où la bonn' femm' chantait,
  Où la bonn' femm' chantait ;
  Dans son joli chant ell' disait
  " Dodo, dodo, dodo, dodo,"
  Et moi qui croyais qu'elle disait
  " Cass' lui les os, cass' lui les os."
  Et moi de m'en cour', cour', cour',
    Et moi de m'en courir !

35

THE OLD MAN IN LEATHER

One mis-ty, mois-ty morn-ing, when clou-dy was the wea-ther, There I met an old man clo-thed all in lea-ther, clo-thed all in lea-ther, With cap un-der his chin, How do you do, how do you do, how do you do, a-gain, a-gain.

AIKEN·DRUM

1. There was a man lived in the moon, lived in the moon, lived in the moon, There was a man lived in the moon, And his name was Ai-kin Drum, And he played up-on a la-dle, a la-dle, a la-dle, And he played up-on a la-dle, And his name was Aikin Drum.

2 And his hat was made of good cream cheese,
And his name, &c.
3 And his coat was made of good roast beef,
And his name, &c.
4 And his buttons were made of penny loaves,
And his name, &c.
5 His waistcoat was made of crust of pies,
And his name, &c.
6 His breeches were made of haggis bags,
And his name, &c.
7 There was a man in another town,
And his name was Willy Wood;

And he played upon a razor.
And his name was Willy Wood.
8 And he ate up all the good cream cheese,
And his name, &c.
9 And he ate up all the good roast beef,
And his name, &c.
10 And he ate up all the penny loaves,
And his name, &c.
11 And he ate up all the good pie crust,
And his name, &c.
12 But he choked upon the haggis bags,
And there was an end of Willy Wood.

BILLY PRINGLE

Bil - ly Prin-gle had a lit-tle pig, When it was young it was not ve-ry big,

When it was old it lived in clover, Now it's dead and that's all o-ver. Bil - ly Pringle

he lay down and died, Bet -ty Prin - gle she lay down and cried, So there was an end of

one, two, and three. Billy Pringle he, Betty Pringle she, and the piggy wiggy wee.

SUR LE PONT D'AVIGNON

Sur le pont d'A-vi-gnon, Tout le mon-de y dan-se, dan-se; Sur le pont d'A-vi-

-gnon, Tout le mon-de y dan-se en rond. Les beaux mes-sieurs font comm' ça,

Et puis en-cor' comm' ça : Sur le pont d'A-vi-gnon, Tout le mon-de y dan-se,

dan-se, Sur le pont d'A-vi-gnon Tout le mon-de y danse en rond.

2 Les belles dames font comm' ça,
Et puis encore comm' ça :
Sur le pont d'Avignon,
Tout le monde y danse, danse,
Sur le pont d'Avignon,
Tout le monde y danse en rond.

3 Et les capucins font comm' ça,
Et puis encore comm' ça :
Sur le pont d'Avignon,
Tout le monde y danse, danse,
Sur le pont d'Avignon,
Tout le monde y danse en rond.

41

LONDON BRIDGE

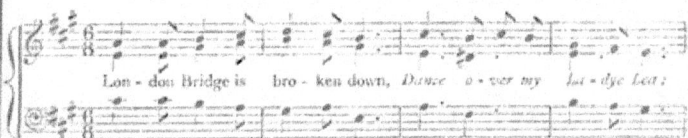

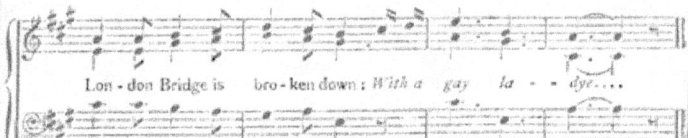

Lon - don Bridge is bro - ken down, *Dance o - ver my la - dye Lea;*

Lon - don Bridge is bro - ken down ; *With a gay la - - dye.…*

2 How shall we build it up again?
   Dance over my Ladye Lea ;
   How shall we build it up again?
   With a gay ladye.

3 Silver and gold will be stole away,
   Dance over my Ladye Lea ;
   Silver and gold will be stole away :
   With a gay ladye.

4 Iron and steel will bend and bow,
   Dance over my Ladye Lea ;

Iron and steel will bend and bow :
   With a gay ladye.

5 Wood and clay will wash away,
   Dance over my Ladye Lea ;
   Wood and clay will wash away :
   With a gay ladye.

6 Build it up with stone so strong,
   Dance over my Ladye Lea ;
   Huzza! 'twill last for ages long,
   With a gay ladye.

CHARLEY·OVER·THE·WATER·

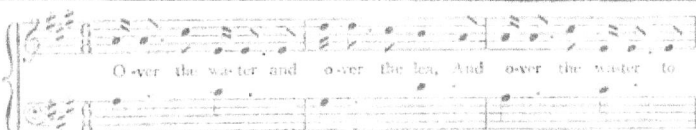

O-ver the wa-ter and o-ver the sea, And o-ver the wa-ter to

Char - ley; And Char - ley loves good ale and wine, And Char - ley loves good

bran - dy, And Charley loves a pret-ty girl As sweet as su - gar candy.

2 Over the water and over the sea,
And over the water to Charley;
I'll have none of your nasty beef,
Nor I'll have none of your barley,
But I'll have some of your very best flour
To make a white cake for my Charley.

43

THE FOUR PRESENTS

I had four bro-thers o-ver the sea, Per-rie, Merrie, Dix-i,
Do-mi-ne: And they each sent a pre-sent un-to me.
Pe-trum, Partrum, Pa-ra-di-si, Tempore, Perrie, Merrie, Dix-i. Do-mi-ne.

2 The first sent a goose without a bone,
 Perrie, Merrie, Dixi, Domine ;
 The second sent a cherry without a stone,
 Petrum, Partrum, Paradisi, Tempore,
 Perrie, Merrie, Dixi, Domine.

3 The third sent a blanket without a thread,
 Perrie, Merrie, Dixi, Domine ;
 The fourth sent a book that no man could
  read,
 Petrum, Partrum, Paradisi, Tempore,
 Perrie, Merrie, Dixi, Domine.

4 When the cherry's in the blossom, there is
  no stone,
 Perrie, Merrie, Dixi, Domine : [no bone.
 When the goose is in the egg-shell, there is
 Petrum, Partrum, Paradisi, Tempore,
 Perrie, Merrie, Dixi, Domine.

5 When the wool's on the sheep's back,
  there's no thread,
 Perrie, Merrie, Dixi, Domine : [can read
 When the book's in the press, no man it
 Petrum, Partrum, Paradisi, Tempore,
 Perrie, Merrie, Dixi, Domine.

44

THE·THREE·LITTLE·KITTENS

There were three lit-tle kit-tens Put on their mit-tens To eat some

Christ-mas pie. *Mew, mew, Mew, mew, Mew, mew, mew.*

2 These three little kittens
They lost their mittens,
And all began to cry.
Mew, mew, &c.

3 " Go, go, naughty kittens,
" And find your mittens,
" Or you shan't have any pie. "
Mew, mew, &c.

4 These three little kittens
They found their mittens,
And joyfully they did cry.
Mew, mew, &c.

5 " O Granny, dear !
" Our mittens are here,
" Make haste and cut up the pie! "
Purr-rr, purr-rr, purr-rr-rr.

PUSSY CAT

Pus - sy - cat high,   Pus - sy - cat low,

Pus - sy - cat was   a fine tea - zer of tow.

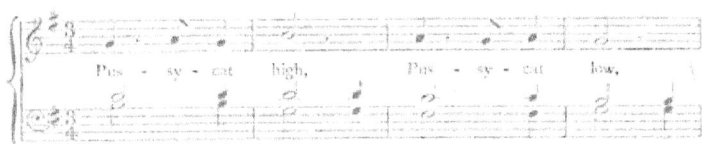

2 Pussy-cat she came into the barn,
  With her bag-pipes under her arm.

3 And then she told a tale to me,
  How Mousey had married a humble bee.

4 Then was I ever so glad,
  That Mousey had married so clever a lad.

ZWEI HASEN

Zwi-schen Berg und tief-en, tief-en Thal, Sas-sen einst zwei Ha-sen,

Fras-sen ab das grü-ne, grü-ne Gras, Fras-sen ab das grü-ne, grü-ne Gras

Bis auf den Ra-sen, Bis..... auf den Ra-sen.

2 Als sie satt gefressen, 'fressen war'n
Setzten sie sich nieder,
Bis und dass der Jäger, Jäger kam,
Und schoss sie nieder, und schoss sie nieder,

3 Als sie sich nun ausgesammelt hatt'n
Und sich befannen,
Dass sie noch Leben, Leben hatt'n
Lasen sie von dannen.

Es reg - net auf der Bru - cke, und ich werd' nass.
Ich bin noch was ver - ges - sen, und weiss nicht was?

Schö - ne Jung - fer hübsch und fein Komm mit mir zum

Tanz he - rein. Lass uns ein - mal tan - zen und lus - tig sein.

LA BERGÈRE

Il é-tait un' ber-gè - re, Et ron, ron, ron, pe-tit pa-ta-pon; Il é-tait
un' ber - gè - re, Qui gar-dait ses mou-tons, Ron, ron, Qui gar-dait ses mou - tons.

2 Elle fit un fromage,
   Et ron, ron, ron, petit patapon ;
   Elle fit un fromage
   Du lait de ses moutons,
   Ron, ron,
   Du lait de ses moutons.

3 Le chat qui la regarde,
   Et ron, ron, ron, petit patapon ;
   Le chat qui la regarde
   D'un petit air fripon,
   Ron, ron,
   D'un petit air fripon.

4 Si tu y mets la patte
   Et ron, ron, ron, petit patapon,
   Si tu y mets la patte
   Tu auras du bâton,
   Ron, ron,
   Tu auras du bâton.

5 Il n'y mit pas la patte,
   Et ron, ron, ron, petit patapon ;
   Il n'y mit pas la patte,
   Il y mit le menton,
   Ron, ron,
   Il y mit le menton.

LE PETIT CHASSEUR

2 Il s'en allait à la chass'.
A la chass' aux z'hannetons;
Quand il fut sur la montagn'
Il partit un coup d' canon.
Et ti, &c.

3 Quand il fut sur la montagn'
Il partit un coup d' canon ;
Il en eut si peur tout d' mêm'
Qu 'il tomba sur ses talons.
Et ti, &c.

4 Il en eut si peur tout d'mêm'
Qu 'il tomba sur ses talons ;
Tout's les dames du villag'
Lui portèrent des bonbons.
Et ti, &c.

5 Tout's les dames du villag'
Lui portèrent des bonbons ;
Je vous remercci', mesdam's,
De vous et de vos bonbons.
Et ti, &c.

Ich ging im Wal - de, So für mich hin, Und

nichts zu su - chen Das war mein Sinn.

2 Im Schatten sah ich
   Ein Blümlein stehn,
   Wie Sterne leuchtend,
   Wie Aeuglein schön.

3 Ich wollt' es brechen
   Da sagt es fein :
   " Soll ich zum Welken
   " Gebrochen sein?"

4 Ich grub's mit allen
   Den Würzlein aus,
   Zum Garten trug ich's
   Am hübschen Haus.

5 Und pflanzt es wieder
   Am stillen Ort ;
   Nun zweigt es immer
   Und blüht so fort.—(Goethe.)

LOOBY LIGHT

Now we dance loo - by, loo - by, loo - by, Now we dance loo -by, loo - by light;

Now we dance loo - by, loo - by, loo - by, Now we dance looby as yes - ter - night.

Shake your right hand a lit-tle, Shake your left hand a lit-tle,

D.C.

Shake your head a lit - tle, And turn you round a - bout.

MARGERY DAW

FORTUNE

See - - saw, Mar - ge - ry Daw Sold her

bed to lie up - on straw; Was - n't she a

dir - ty slut To sell her bed and lie up - on dirt?

THE FLY & THE HUMBLE BEE

Fid - dle - de - dee, Fid - dle - de - dee, The fly has mar - ried the hum - ble bee. Says the fly, says he, "Will you mar - ry me, And live with me, Sweet hum - ble bee?"

2 Says the bee, says she,
"I'll live under your wing,
"And you'll never know
"That I carry a sting."
Fiddle-de-dee, &c.

3 So when the parson
Had joined the pair,
They both went out
To take the air.
Fiddle-de-dee, &c.

4 And the flies did buzz,
And the bells did ring—
Did ever you hear
So merry a thing?
Fiddle-de-dee, &c.

5 And then to think
That of all the flies
The humble bee
Should carry the prize.
Fiddle-de-dee, &c.

www.ingramcontent.com/pod-product-compliance
Lightning Source LLC
Chambersburg PA
CBHW021643270326
41931CB00008B/1148